Women Who Win

Cynthia Cooper

Mia Hamm

Martina Hingis

Chamique Holdsclaw

Michelle Kwan

Lisa Leslie

Sheryl Swoopes

Venus & Serena Williams

CHELSEA HOUSE PUBLISHERS

WOMEN WHO WIN

MICHELLE KWAN

Sherry Beck Paprocki

Introduction by
HANNAH STORM

CHELSEA HOUSE PUBLISHERS
Philadelphia

Frontis: *Figure skater Michelle Kwan's artistry on the ice has won her national and international championships and made her one of the top skaters in the world.*

Produced by
21st Century Publishing and Communications, Inc.
New York, New York
http://www.21cpc.com

CHELSEA HOUSE PUBLISHERS

Editor in Chief: Stephen Reginald
Managing Editor: James D. Gallagher
Production Manager: Pamela Loos
Art Director: Sara Davis
Director of Photography: Judy L. Hasday
Senior Production Editor: J. Christopher Higgins
Publishing Coordinator: James McAvoy
Project Editor: Anne Hill

The Chelsea House World Wide Web address is
http://www.chelseahouse.com

First Printing

1 3 5 7 9 8 6 4 2

Library of Congress Cataloging-in-Publication Data

Paprocki, Sherry.
  Michelle Kwan / Sherry Paprocki.
  p. cm. – (Women who win)
  Includes bibliographical references (p.) and index.
  Summary: A biography of the Chinese-American figure skater known for her artistry on the ice.
  ISBN 0-7910-5792-5 (hc) — ISBN 0-7910-6152-3 (pbk)
  1. Kwan, Michelle, 1980– —Juvenile literature. 2. Skaters—United States—Biography—Juvenile literature. 3. Women skaters—United States—Biography—Juvenile literature. [1. Kwan, Michelle, 1980– 2. Ice skaters. 3. Chinese Americans—Biography. 4. Women—Biography] I. Title. II. Series.

GV850.K93 P26 2000
796.91'2'092—dc21
[B]   00—029041
                                                                         CIP
                                                                          AC

CONTENTS

WOMEN WHO WIN

Hannah Storm
NBC Studio Host

You go girl! Women's sports are the hottest thing going right now, with the 1900s ending in a big way. When the U.S. team won the 1999 Women's World Cup, it captured the imagination of all sports fans and served as a great inspiration for young girls everywhere to follow their dreams.

That was just the exclamation point on an explosive decade for women's sports—capped off by the Olympic gold medals for the U.S. women in hockey, softball, and basketball. All the excitement created by the U.S. national basketball team helped to launch the Women's National Basketball Association (WNBA), which began play in 1997. The fans embraced the concept, and for the first time, a successful and stable women's professional basketball league was formed.

I was the first ever play-by-play announcer for the WNBA—a big personal challenge. Broadcasting, just like sports, had some areas with limited opportunities for women. There have traditionally not been many play-by-play opportunities for women in sports television, so I had no experience. To tell you the truth, the challenge I faced was a little scary! Sometimes we are all afraid that we might not be up to a certain task. It is not easy to take risks, but unless we push ourselves we will stagnate and not grow.

Here's what happened to me. I had always wanted to do play-by-play earlier in my career, but I had never gotten the opportunity. Not that I was unhappy— I had been given studio hosting assignments that were unprecedented for a woman and my reputation was well established in the business. I was comfortable in my role . . . plus I had just had my first baby. The last thing I needed to do was suddenly tackle a new skill on national television and risk being criticized (not to mention, very stressed out!). Although I had always wanted to do play-by-play, I turned down the assignment twice, before reluctantly agreeing to give it a try. During my hosting stint of the NBA finals that year, I traveled back and forth to WNBA preseason games to practice play-by-play. I was on 11 flights in 14 days to seven different cities! My head was spinning and it was no surprise that I got sick. On the day of the first broadcast, I had to have shots just so I could go on the air without throwing up. I felt terrible and nervous, but

I survived my first game. I wasn't very good but gradually, week by week, I got better. By the end of the season, the TV reviews of my work were much better— *USA Today* called me "most improved."

During that 1997 season, I witnessed a lot of exciting basketball moments, from the first historic game to the first championship, won by the Houston Comets. The challenge of doing play-by-play was really exciting and I loved interviewing the women athletes and seeing the fans' enthusiasm. Over one million fans came to the games; my favorite sight was seeing young boys wearing the jerseys of female players—pretty cool. And to think I almost missed out on all of that. It reinforced the importance of taking chances and not being afraid of challenges or criticism. When we have an opportunity to follow our dreams, we need to go for it!

Thankfully, there are now more opportunities than ever for women in sports (and other areas, like broadcasting). We thank women, like those in this series, who have persevered despite lack of opportunities—women who have refused to see their limitations. Remember, women's sports has been around a long time. Way back in 396 B.C. Kyniska, a Spartan princess, won an Olympic chariot race. Of course, women weren't allowed to compete, so she was not allowed to collect her prize in person. At the 1996 Olympic games in Atlanta, Georgia, over 35,600 women competed, almost a third more than in the previous Summer Games. More than 20 new women's events have been added for the Sydney, Australia, Olympics in 2000. Women's collegiate sports continues to grow, spurred by the 1972 landmark legislation Title IX, which states that "no person in the United States shall, on the basis of sex, be excluded from participation in, be denied the benefits of, or be subjected to discrimination under any educational program or activity receiving federal financial assistance." This has set the stage for many more scholarships and opportunities for women, and now we have professional leagues as well. No longer do the most talented basketball players in the country have to go to Europe or Asia to earn a living.

The women in this series did not have as many opportunities as you have today. But they were persistent through all obstacles, both on the court and off. I can tell you that Cynthia Cooper is the strongest woman I know. What is it that makes Cynthia and the rest of the women included in this series so special? They are not afraid to share their struggles and their stories with us. Their willingness to show us their emotions, open their hearts, bare their souls, and let us into their lives is what, in my mind, separates them from their male counterparts. So accept this gift of their remarkable stories and be inspired. Because *you*, too, have what it takes to follow your dreams.

1

SETTING A
HIGH STANDARD

The soft music of "Lyra Angelica" ("Song of the Angels") played as figure skater Michelle Kwan floated across the ice at the rink in Philadelphia, Pennsylvania. She was competing in the 1998 U.S. National Figure Skating Championship, the event that guarantees spots on the U.S. Olympic team.

Dressed in a sky-blue costume, Michelle was light on her skates, spinning her way to a first-place finish that evening. During the competition she focused on her dream—skating at the upcoming 1998 Olympic Games in Nagano, Japan.

Michelle was warmed by the many smiling faces in the audience as fans waved signs from the stands, encouraging her to do her best. When she finished her performance, she skated to her coach, Frank Carroll, and hugged him. Michelle knew she had done well.

Michelle had already set a high standard for herself and the rest of the world's ice skaters. Earlier in the competition, she had earned seven 6.0s (perfect scores) in the short program, the technical part of the competition

At the U.S. National Figure Skating Championship in 1998, Michelle performed brilliantly. The high standards she set for herself earned her first place and a guaranteed spot at the Olympics.

during which all skaters are required to perform certain moves. Judges are notoriously tough in scoring these programs, which account for one-third of the total score. Michelle was the first woman in the history of the U.S. Nationals to win perfect scores in a short program.

The long program, or free skate, counts as two-thirds of a skater's scores. The free skate allows individual skaters more creativity to perform moves that they choose. When the nine judges' scores appeared for Michelle's long program, she was thrilled. Eight of the judges gave her 6.0s. Again, she made history. Never before had any U.S. female figure skater received eight 6.0s for a long program. "She found something out about herself," her choreographer, Lori Nichol, told a reporter from *Sports Illustrated.* "She learned she could feel serenity and joy on the ice, in front of a crowd, in an incredibly pressurized moment."

Michelle's wondrous performance at the Nationals gave the young champion a boost toward the Olympics, which were just six weeks away. She was nervous but still confident that her program featuring "Lyra Angelica" would help her do well.

Michelle had a problem during those weeks, however. Prior to the Nationals, she had broken the second toe on her left foot. Intensely concentrated as she jumped and spiraled to win the U.S. title, she often did not even notice the injury. Still, it did create a problem, which became more evident during practice for the Olympic competition. Her doctor told her to begin physical therapy and to rest, a difficult task for a champion skater.

Six weeks later, Michelle's broken toe kept her from going to the opening ceremonies for

Michelle and her coach, Frank Carroll, erupt in shouts and applause at learning Michelle had earned eight perfect scores for her long program at the 1998 Nationals. An observer said of her incredible skating, "Michelle's capable of doing these types of performances more than once."

the Olympic Games, and she watched them on television before she left the United States. When she finally arrived in Nagano, she nearly cried when she saw the Olympic rings, the symbol of the games. From the time she was a little girl, Michelle had dreamed of competing in the Olympics. Now she was just 17 and her dream was finally coming true.

Reporters crowded around the ice during Michelle's first practice, and the national network CBS filmed the practice as part of its Olympic coverage. Even though Michelle had jet lag after a day of flying to Japan, she ran through her four-minute program without stopping. She fell once during her opening jump, a triple lutz, but performed beautifully in the rest of her practice.

During the next several days, Michelle continued to work on her routine. Although her toe was not completely healed, she skated as though she had no injury. Instead of staying in the Olympic village with the rest of the athletes, Michelle stayed at a hotel in Nagano with her mother so that she could be well rested when it was her time to compete.

Michelle knew the competition was tough. Her U.S. teammate Tara Lipinski, who was only 15 years old, was her strongest competitor. Some observers said that Michelle and Tara were leaps and bounds ahead of the other skaters. Still it was hard to compete against someone who was on the same team.

Nine days after she arrived in Nagano, Michelle placed first for her short program. The crowd was crazy about her. "I'd heard everybody scream and cheer and I thought, 'God, it was like I was in heaven,'" she told the *Boston Globe*.

Tara finished second in the short program. Now both skaters knew that either of them could take home the gold two days later with the free-skate competition, and Michelle was under a lot of pressure. Many people expected her to win, and judges and observers scrutinized each of her practices, trying to guess how she would do during the free skate.

Michelle was apprehensive about the long program, afraid she would disappoint her family and friends. The day before the program, however, she was upbeat and confident. Michelle Kwan was ready to go for the gold.

Confident in her abilities and cheered by her fans, Michelle performs a graceful turn at the 1998 Olympics.

Each of the skaters had drawn numbers earlier to determine the order in which they would perform. Michelle was the first on the rink, and as she ventured onto the ice, the crowd went wild, loudly cheering her entrance. Through the noise, she reminded herself of the philosophy she had practiced since she started skating at age six: "Work hard, be yourself and have fun."

2

A DETERMINED FAMILY

Michelle's parents, Estella and Danny Kwan, were born in China and emigrated to the United States in the 1970s. When they met and married, they made their home in southern California, where Michelle and her brother and sister were born. Estella and Danny were hard-working parents who were determined to do everything possible to help their children pursue their dreams.

Danny Kwan was born in a small village near the city of Canton, now called Guangzhou, in southeastern China. Life in the village was difficult for the Kwans and their children, and two months before Danny was born, his father was forced to leave their home to find work elsewhere. Danny remembered how hard it was for his family to make ends meet. While Michelle was growing up he often told her stories about life in China and how hard he had worked in his village to help his mother and his brothers and sisters survive.

Finally, when Danny was eight years old, his father got a job in Hong Kong, a large city off the southern coast of

Michelle shares a happy moment with her grandfather Ho Yuen Kwan. Michelle's determination to be a champion skater was matched by the determination of her family to help her realize that dream. Their encouragement and support played a major role in her success at such a young age.

When Michelle's father, Danny, was growing up in China, his life in a small village like this one was difficult. As a boy, he struggled to help his family make ends meet, and when he came to the United States, he worked hard to provide opportunities and a better life for his children.

China. The Kwan family moved to Hong Kong, where the young boy first attended school. Because Danny had waited so long before starting school, he had a lot of catching up to do, and he was eager to learn. He did, however, have enough time to notice a young girl in his classroom. Her name was Estella.

Estella, who had lived in Hong Kong all her life, had a happy childhood surrounded by a large family of several brothers and sisters. She was one of the smartest students in the class, and besides enjoying school, she also loved music and ballet.

An ambitious boy, Danny not only worked hard at his studies but also took a job as a messenger when he was 13 years old. Later, he worked for a telephone company. By the time Danny was 21, he had finished school and was looking ahead to the future. At the time, he didn't know his future lay in the United States.

Danny first visited the United States in 1971, when he traveled to California to attend a relative's wedding. The young man saw so many opportunities in America that he decided to stay. The first thing he had to do was find a job, and he found work in a restaurant, learning to be a cook. Danny had so much energy, however, that he also took a second job at Pacific Bell, a local telephone company, where he was a systems analyst. Before long, Danny and a partner opened their own restaurant, called the Golden Pheasant, in Torrance, California, a town south of Los Angeles.

After Danny had left Hong Kong, he did not see Estella again for many years. After she had finished school, she became a nurse and worked in a local hospital. Eventually, Estella changed careers and became a television anchor woman reporting the news in Hong Kong. By the time Danny saw her again, Estella was regularly appearing on television.

The couple finally got together when Danny returned to Hong Kong for a school reunion. Soon after, they were married, and Estella moved to Torrance with Danny, whose parents also emigrated to America. Danny, Estella, and his parents all worked together at the Golden Pheasant.

In 1976, Danny and Estella became the proud parents of their first child, a son they named Ron. Two years later a baby girl, Karen, entered the family. Then, the Kwans were surprised and pleased to learn that Estella was pregnant once again. On July 7, 1980, another baby girl was born. They named her Michelle.

Danny and Estella knew they would have to work hard to take care of their growing family, but they could not know the special interests that their children would develop in the coming years. Young Ron was the first in the family to start ice skating, joining a hockey team that practiced at a rink near the Kwan home. Watching Ron gliding on the ice, competing hard with his teammates, Michelle fell in love with the idea of ice skating. Only five years old, she began asking her parents to let her take lessons.

Although Danny and Estella thought Michelle was far too young to learn how to skate, she pleaded and sometimes cried, and her parents finally gave in. She could learn to skate. Karen too wanted to skate, and the two sisters, laced up in old brown skates they rented from the rink, made their first attempt on the ice. Just standing up on the skates was not easy, but before long Michelle felt quite comfortable, and she began skating regularly at a rink in the Rolling Hills Estates shopping mall, not far from her home.

"My first skating memory is from when I was six," Michelle told a reporter when she was nearly 15 years old. "I was wearing rental skates and eating Nerds candy."

Determined to be a good skater, Michelle, along with Karen, took group lessons once a

week. One of the first moves the girls learned was how to fall down. Michelle wasn't very patient, however. Racing around the rink, she loved the way it felt sailing across the ice, and she was eager, even as a beginner, to learn fancy moves.

Soon Michelle and Karen were taking private lessons, learning the basics of ice skating, including pushing off with one foot, gliding, and skating forward and backward. Michelle, however, wanted to learn more, and she decided to

Whenever Michelle fell, she was quick to recover and jump to her feet. Long hours of practice and concentration were essential to perfect her moves on the ice.

try leaping into the air. Because she was so tiny, spinning above the ice was easy for the young skater, and although she sometimes fell, she was always quick to jump up. Michelle's lessons in learning how to fall were an important experience; they taught her how not to get hurt when taking a tumble on the cold, hard ice.

Michelle's early determination to be the best skater kept her reaching for her goal. Extremely focused when she skated, she always wanted to do more. As soon as she learned something new, she was eager to know what was next, constantly asking her teacher for new and greater challenges.

Michelle and Karen are not only sisters but good friends as well, and they spent many hours together on the rink. They showed each other drills and moves and practiced together. Through their practice and skating sessions, their skills gradually improved, and as the sisters became well-known at the rink, they felt it was time for them to have their own ice skates. The girls had learned a lot about different blade positions, and they wanted the best equipment possible.

Eager to practice their new skills with shiny new blades, Michelle and Karen finally persuaded their parents to help them choose their own skates. They selected white boots, with blades that were not too deep or shallow, and because the girls' feet were still growing, they didn't get the most expensive blades. Instead, they bought skates that would support their ankles well but were reasonably priced. Estella and Danny knew it would not be long until both daughters outgrew their skates and would have to buy new pairs.

The Kwans were learning that skating was an expensive hobby. Purchasing skates and paying for ongoing lessons and time for the girls to practice on the rink was costly. Estella and Danny did not begrudge the expense, however. They understood how important skating was to Michelle and Karen, and they sacrificed to make their daughters' dreams a reality.

3

NOT TOO YOUNG
TO DREAM

Michelle stared at the television, mesmerized by the man gliding across the ice. The scene was the 1988 Winter Olympics in Calgary, Canada, and she was watching Brian Boitano. She stared in awe as he skated so elegantly in his blue costume to the militant music of "Napoleon and Josephine."

Boitano's performance absolutely amazed Michelle. Even though she was only seven years old, she admired his strength, power, and enthusiasm. For Michelle, Boitano's gold medal that year was a tremendous thrill, and his performance was an inspiration. She vowed to dedicate herself to the pursuit of her dream. Practicing at the rink, she exerted energy the way she thought Boitano would during his practices.

Determined to know what it felt like to win an Olympic gold medal, Michelle promised herself that one day she would find out. Counting the years ahead, she decided that she wanted to be at the Olympics in 1994, 1998, 2002, and even 2006. By that year, she would be 26 years old. The Olympics were far away from her hometown rink,

---

Only a child when she became enthralled with skating, Michelle began to pursue her goal of one day reaching the Olympics. She had to take lessons, practice, and enter skating competitions in order to realize that dream.

however, and Michelle was growing bored with her lessons. She did learn some difficult moves, such as a single axel, in which she spun in the air one-and-a-half times and then landed on the opposite foot. Still, Michelle's hunger could not be satisfied, and she continued to beg her instructor for greater challenges.

The Kwans realized that if the girls were to develop their skills, they needed more professional training than their local rink could provide. Searching for an instructor, Danny found Derek James, who taught at another rink near their home and conducted a disciplined training program. Soon, the excited young skaters were training with Derek five days a week. Their new schedule was demanding. They had to be at the skating rink by 5:30 A.M. for a couple of hours of lessons and practice before school started. Then they met with Derek again after school as well as on Wednesday evenings.

Derek saw the girls' great potential, and he encouraged Michelle and Karen to join the Ice Skating Institute of America and the United States Figure Skating Association (USFSA). As members of USFSA, they could participate in skating competitions. For Michelle, it was the first step toward the Olympics.

Estella and Danny knew their two daughters were talented, and they also felt that skating was an excellent outlet for their self-expression. They were concerned, however, that the girls have as normal lives as possible and encouraged them to enjoy other activities. The Kwans made sure that there was enough free time for Michelle and Karen to play games together. Michelle loved her stuffed animals and also collected stamps.

Skating, however, was the girls' first love, but the more practice and skating they did, the more expensive it became. If the young hopefuls were going to enter competitions, they would need professional skates, impressive costumes, and still more time on the ice. The Kwans were aware that sacrifices were necessary if Michelle and Karen were to realize their dreams, and the entire family pitched in to help. Extra money for other fun activities was sometimes scarce, but the girls didn't seem to mind as long as they could skate.

Danny continued working for the telephone company while Estella worked in the family restaurant. For a time, she took a factory job as well. Even so, sometimes the Kwans did not have enough money for the girls' lessons with Derek. Michelle and Karen still kept up their skating, however. Remembering the stories of how difficult it was for her father and grandfather when they were children and how they did not have the opportunities she had, Michelle worked even harder to improve her skills.

Michelle was also serious about her schoolwork. Along with Karen and Ron, she made sure to keep up with her classes, even though

Michelle and Karen (in front) were more than just sisters. They were also close friends who practiced, trained, and entered competitions together as they were growing up.

she spent hours at the rink. She liked school and enjoyed the friends she met there, but her best friend while she was growing up was her sister. Karen and Michelle practiced together at the skating rink and even learned each other's programs.

Although the closest of friends, Michelle and Karen differ physically and in their skating style. Karen, at 5' 8", is much taller than Michelle, who is only 5' 2". At the rink, observers and other skaters called them "Big Kwan" and "Little Kwan." Because of her sister's height, Michelle always seemed to feel that Karen looked much more elegant than herself when she skated, and she worked hard to imitate Karen's grace on the ice. Michelle's style was more athletic than Karen's, however, and the younger skater was also more competitive. She never seemed satisfied with her results in a skating competition unless she won the gold medal.

While the girls were taking lessons from Derek, they almost never missed practices. They were at the rink nearly every day and entered many skating competitions. The USFSA sponsors events on several levels: preprelimi-nary, preliminary, prejuvenile, juvenile, inter-mediate, novice, junior, and senior. Skaters who are bound for the Olympics skate at the senior level, and it takes a great deal of effort and concentration to achieve that level.

As Michelle continued her training, she would not be satisfied until she learned all the most difficult moves. Practice, practice, and more practice began to pay off; she won her first gold medal in competition when she was seven years old. After that, she and Karen both began winning awards in competitions. When the girls were not working on their competitive programs, they were taking skating tests so they could move up to higher levels in the USFSA.

By the time Michelle was 11 years old, she was skating at the junior level. In 1992, she won a gold medal at the Southwest Pacific Regionals and then a bronze medal at the Pacific Coast Sectionals, which qualified her to go on to the Junior National Championships. Michelle had come this far without ever having had a full-time coach.

What the Kwan sisters did have was many relatives who supported their skating ambitions. Michelle's parents, grandparents, and many aunts, uncles, and cousins encouraged her to pursue her dream. When her grandmother gave her a gold pendant in the form of a dragon—a Chinese symbol for good luck—Michelle began wearing it in all her competitions. Even as she skated in the Olympics, the gold pendant dangled from her neck.

As Michelle and Karen moved closer to their Olympic goal, expenses mounted, and Danny and Estella made an extremely difficult decision. To raise money, they decided to sell their home and move in with Danny's parents. The entire Kwan family was determined to help Michelle achieve her Olympic dream.

4

STUDYING AT ICE CASTLE

Derek James knew that both Kwan sisters had tremendous potential. He also knew that they were ready for more advanced training than he could provide. Meanwhile, Michelle took pride in the fact that she was in the junior division despite not having a full-time coach. Although she and Karen practiced as much as possible at the Torrance rink, ice hockey teams booked a lot of time on weekends, and the Kwans began looking for other options.

Estella and Danny had heard about and were somewhat familiar with the Ice Castle International Training Center, a place nestled in the San Bernardino Mountains at Lake Arrowhead. Driving to the Ice Castle, the Kwans arranged to stay at a friend's vacation home on weekends so their daughters could have more time to practice there. As the girls skated at the Ice Castle's public rink, Michelle loved to look out at the giant pine trees that encircled the partially enclosed rink.

Tucked deeper into the mountains at the Ice Castle

Michelle's serious training began when she attended the Ice Castle International Training Center and became a full-time student of coach Frank Carroll, here guiding the young skater. With Coach Carroll, Michelle kept a busy schedule of practice, training, and studies, and her confidence in her abilities grew.

was another rink, a private rink where many professional skaters worked with their coaches. Some of the best figure skaters in the world trained there, including World Champion Lu Chen and many others. Michelle dreamed of floating around that exclusive rink, and getting the chance to share the ice with these great skaters. Perhaps it was these dreams that propelled her to practice and train even harder.

The Ice Castle was not just a practice ground for Michelle and Karen. It was the place where doors were soon to open for the girls when they met a woman named Virginia Fratianne, whose daughter, Linda Fratianne, was a well-known skater from the 1970s. It was Virginia Fratianne who saw the girls' talents and introduced them to a coach named Frank Carroll. Michelle and Karen knew that Carroll had coached Linda Fratianne and many other world-class figure skaters, and they desperately hoped he would agree to become their trainer.

First, however, they had to skate for Frank, and they were nervous about performing for such a famous coach. When Michelle stepped onto the ice, she immediately forgot her jitters, and her confidence quickly returned. After their performances, Frank agreed to take them on as students. Michelle and Karen were ecstatic.

Time was very short, however. The Junior National Championships were only three weeks away, and Michelle would have to train seriously. Karen had already skated at a national competition the year before, in the novice class, but this was Michelle's first opportunity. She was surprised at what she accomplished in the next three weeks as Frank

*World champion Lu
Chen of China is
a dazzling skater.
Watching her train and
perform encouraged
Michelle to work even
harder to reach her
goal of becoming a
world champion
as well.*

helped her prepare. Michelle admitted that she
had developed a lot of bad skating habits, and
Frank helped her get rid of them. He also
taught her how to get up and continue skating
every time she fell. It felt like she was already
practicing for the Olympics.

Finally, the time arrived, and Michelle was
on her way to her first national competition.
Arriving in Florida, she was amazed at what
she saw. She was one of the youngest skaters
there; some junior competitors were more than
20 years old. Michelle was also dazzled by the
glitzy costumes and the makeup the competitors wore. (Michelle would not begin wearing

makeup until a few years later.)

When it was time for her to take to the ice, Michelle was convinced that she would float through her program as she had done at the sectionals. She was wrong. Finishing ninth in the competition, the disappointed 11-year-old broke down in tears. She had learned a lot, however, and began to realize that she had probably been too confident. She thought she would skate as smoothly as she had in past competitions, but now she knew she had to work even harder on every aspect of her skating if she was going to succeed.

For Michelle and Karen, becoming full-time students at Ice Castle meant they could finally skate on the private rink. Michelle's goal of being on the ice with the world's best figure skaters was going to be realized. The sisters also received scholarships that allowed them to live at Ice Castle and skate there seven days a week.

Michelle loved living at Ice Castle, where she and Karen shared a cabin with their father, who drove back and forth to work every day. She also appreciated the fact that her schoolwork was organized around her skating practices. Most of all, however, she loved being so close to a rink that was nearly always available for practice.

For Michelle's family, however, the situation was not that easy. Estella stayed in Torrance with Ron so that he could graduate from high school and work at the family restaurant. She traveled to Lake Arrowhead on the weekends. Danny's trip to and from work was nearly two hours each way. "Our family has gotten used to it," Estella once told a reporter. "But it's a sacrifice."

At Ice Castle, for the first time in her life, Michelle saw the commitment and dedication of the world's best skaters. The top figure skaters working there focused on every aspect of their skating, from the way they moved their heads to the way they completed their jumps and spins. She was amazed, and thrilled, at their determination.

During her first two years at Lake Arrowhead, Michelle went to school during the day and skated before and after classes. When she was 12, however, she stopped formally attending classes. Instead, a teacher delivered assignments to her on Wednesdays, and Michelle did all her schoolwork during the week, turning it in to the visiting teacher the following Wednesday. "I needed more lessons from my coach, so I decided to do independent studies," she told a reporter from the *Los Angeles Times*.

Michelle followed a busy skating schedule. She awoke at 6:45 A.M. each day for breakfast and had a skating lesson an hour later. From 9:30 A.M. to noon, she studied and then had lunch. After lunch, at 2 P.M., she took another skating lesson, and at 3:15 P.M. she had time for a short nap. At 4:30 P.M. she went to her third skating lesson of the day. Dinner was at 5:20 P.M., followed by weight training and cardiovascular exercise to help her control her breathing when she skated. She was in bed by 8:00 every evening.

As Michelle's confidence in her skating ability grew, she knew she could do all the necessary jumps and wanted desperately to move up to the senior division. Frank told her to wait a while before she tested because she still needed more practice. He also knew how very difficult the competition was at this most advanced level. Michelle could not wait, however. Instead she ignored Frank's advice and decided that she would try to meet the goal her father had set for her five years earlier. Without talking to Frank beforehand, she took the test, and just a few months before she turned 12, Michelle reached the highest level of amateur skating. She passed the test to become a senior skater.

Frank was angry that Michelle had not listened to him, and his anger surprised Danny. He thought Michelle had talked it over with her coach. Later, Danny told a *Sports Illustrated* reporter that it was all a mistake. "We'd only known Frank for four months and I thought Michelle had told him about it," he said. "The only thing she wanted was to be a senior and compete against the big guys."

Finally, Michelle was among the top skaters in the world and was pushing herself hard because she wanted to be in the Olympics, which were just two years away. When Frank told her she would have to work twice as hard or she would embarrass herself, Michelle took his advice to heart. "I like my schedule to be jam-packed," she once told a reporter. "I didn't want to finish my homework and watch four hours of TV. I wanted to get to the 1994 Olympics."

The year before the Olympics, in 1993, Michelle was the youngest senior competitor the national competition judges had seen in 20 years. She finished in sixth place. A few months later she went to the Olympic Festival in San Antonio, Texas, and won the competition there. Later that year she was allowed to participate in the World Junior Championships

Only 13 years old, Michelle performs at the Olympic Festival in San Antonio, Texas. When she won the competition, she was well on her way to participating in the Olympics.

in Colorado and skated so well she became the World Junior Champion!

People were surprised at this new, young skater on the ice. She was so tiny. At the time she was less than 5' tall and she weighed less than 100 pounds. Yet Michelle was absolutely determined. Only a few people knew that her real dream was to participate in the next year's Olympic competition.

5

A STRANGE YEAR

On a snowy January day in 1994, Michelle witnessed one of the most startling events of her skating life. Waiting in the wings for her turn to perform at the 1994 U.S. National Championships in Detroit, Michigan, she heard a scream. It was a moment that ice skating fans around the world will never forget.

Michelle was only 13 years old, but she can still clearly remember what happened. She and defending U.S. champion Nancy Kerrigan were in the same practice group on the rink prior to competition. A great many people thought Nancy would win the national championship for the second year in a row, and those watching her practice believed she was the best.

As Michelle was leaving the rink, she heard someone ask for Nancy's autograph, and Michelle stepped aside, letting Nancy walk ahead of her. A few minutes after Nancy disappeared behind a curtain, Michelle heard her scream. A crowd of people frantically pushed past Michelle, who thought Nancy had fallen. Later Michelle found out that Nancy had been struck on the left knee, on

Nineteen ninety-four was a memorable year for the skating world, which was rocked by the assault on Nancy Kerrigan, shown here at a press conference. For Michelle, it was also memorable because she was asked to attend the Olympics as an alternate skater.

purpose, by a man carrying a tire iron. Michelle watched in awe as the media swarmed into the arena to cover the story, which made headlines on most every news broadcast.

Because of the injury, Nancy was forced out of the competition, but other fine U.S. skaters remained, among them Tonya Harding, who was a strong competitor to Nancy Kerrigan. Other contenders included Nicole Bobek, Elaine Zayak, and Lisa Ervin, all of whom were a lot older than Michelle.

Although the commotion around the assault on Nancy confused and upset Michelle, she did well during the competition. She finished second with the silver medal; Tonya Harding won the gold medal. Michelle was thrilled because the U.S. Nationals is the qualifier that determines which figure skaters go to the Olympics, and she thought she might be one of them.

Her hopes were dashed, however, when the U.S. Figure Skating Association decided that Nancy Kerrigan deserved a shot at the Olympics. Since there was only room for two figure skaters on the team, Nancy and Tonya Harding were chosen to represent the United States. In spite of her disappointment, Michelle thought the choice was fair. She felt that if Nancy had not been injured, she might very well have won the gold medal.

As the weeks passed, rumors and suspicions about the attack on Nancy began to escalate. The U.S. Olympic Committee (USOC) and others began questioning whether Tonya Harding could have had a role in the incident. The committee considered disqualifying Tonya from the competition but finally concluded that there was simply not enough hard evidence to justify such a decision.

To her surprise, Michelle was named the first alternate for the Olympics and was told by USOC officials to get ready to fly to Lillehammer, Norway. No one really knew if Michelle would actually skate at Lillehammer, but the media went wild anyway. Reporters showed up at Ice Castle pressing for interviews with her, and television stations called incessantly. It was Michelle's first time in the spotlight, and her parents and coach Frank Carroll were not sure how to handle the attention.

Danny and Estella decided they needed help, and they called a sports manager named Shep Goldberg, who lived in Michigan. Shep represented many other athletes, and Michelle's parents thought he would know how to deal with the media. Shep flew straight to Lake Arrowhead and quickly brought the situation under control.

The Kwan family was filled with anxiety. They knew Michelle had great opportunities ahead of her, but being an alternate to the Olympics during all this controversy was difficult for everyone. Michelle focused on her skating and eagerly looked forward to her trip. She practiced as though she knew she would be competing, even getting a private tutor instead of continuing in eighth grade.

Although Michelle had dreamed of going to the 1994 Olympics, she never thought it would happen quite this way. As she packed her suitcase and prepared to go, she still had no idea whether or not she would skate.

Still, she was hoping she would get the chance to perform as she headed to Lillehammer with her dad and coach. Once they arrived, Michelle did not go to the Olympic village but instead stayed in a nearby hotel. Because she

Michelle talks with a reporter about the 1994 Olympics. Because of the controversy over the assault on Nancy Kerrigan, skating was suddenly tops in the news. The media lavished attention on figure skaters, including Michelle, who was besieged by requests for interviews.

was not an official member of the Olympic team, she was not allowed to practice with the other skaters. When the day of competition came, it was Nancy and Tonya who represented the United States.

Michelle watched the competition from the stands and cheered for both U.S. skaters. Despite her injury, Nancy's performance was brilliant, and she won the silver medal. Tonya did not do well, finishing eighth. Sixteen-year-old Oksana Baiul from the Ukraine won the gold medal.

By the time the Olympics were over, officials had found evidence that Tonya was linked to the attack on Nancy. Eventually, the USFSA banned Tonya from ever skating again in Olympic-type competitions. It was discovered that both Tonya's husband and her bodyguard were involved in the incident, and a court found Tonya guilty of trying to interfere in the investigation of the attack. She was fined $160,000, given three years' probation, and ordered to perform 500 hours of community service.

Following Lillehammer, Nancy Kerrigan left amateur skating and turned professional; and Tonya Harding was also out of amateur competitions. The entire incident, however, drew a great deal of attention to the sport. Figure skating became immensely popular, drawing more and more fans. "It's absolutely mind-boggling how figure skating became so popular because of that incident," Michelle's coach, Frank, told a reporter from the *New York Times* a few years later.

Terrible and regrettable though the incident was, it helped propel Michelle even further into the spotlight. When it was time to compete in the World Championships, Michelle was the only U.S. representative that year. Only 13 years old, she was the youngest person to ever skate for the United States in world competition. A great many people were concerned that it was too much pressure on someone so young.

6

A WORLD WINNER

Pressure could not stop an excited Michelle from working toward her goal. She practiced and trained extremely hard, even spending extra time with other coaches. When she finally entered the World Championships, she was a bit too nervous and did not do well in her technical program. Specifically, her triple lutz (a jump that takes off on a back outside edge, with three revolutions in the air before again landing on a back outside edge) caused some problems. She placed 11th in that part of the program. It was important for her future that she place in the top 10. If she did not, the United States would not have two spots for skaters to attend the Worlds the following year. Michelle and Frank tried not to focus on all that added pressure.

When Michelle stepped onto the ice to skate her long program, the audience roared. Thrilled at her fans' support, she was determined to do her best. Her program was excellent, including her two tricky triple lutzes. In the end, Michelle was in the top 10, having taken eighth place.

An exultant Michelle waves the American flag after winning the World Championship in 1996 in Edmonton, Canada. She had not wavered in her determination to win, and her performance and the new image she projected won her the women's figure skating title.

Michelle's skating career was thriving as she participated in skating competitions all around the country in the summer of 1994. It seemed everyone wanted her to make an appearance. Accompanied by her mother, she traveled with Campbell Soup's Tour of World Figure Skating Champions. For Michelle it was a tremendous thrill because she got to perform with her idol, Brian Boitano, as well as Oksana Baiul, who was also skating with the tour. That summer they skated in 76 ice shows.

Even though Michelle loved skating with all of the Olympic champions, her focus was on the next year. She was determined that she would be one of the two U.S. figure skaters competing at the 1995 World Championships. Many people would have agreed that she was in top form and would likely be the next figure skating star. Reporters from newspapers, magazines, and television clamored for interviews. *Sports Illustrated* wrote about her and so did *Seventeen* and *People* magazines.

Finally, it was time for the U.S. Nationals, held in Providence, Rhode Island, and Michelle felt she was ready. Karen was also skating in her first national competition, and the sisters enjoyed themselves immensely during the trip.

Although many people thought Michelle would win, the older Nicole Bobek took home the gold. The competition between the two was close, but Michelle had fallen when she was doing a triple lutz in her program. She placed second, taking home the silver.

The young skater looked ahead optimistically to the next event, the Worlds in Birmingham, England. Even though Frank had made Michelle's program harder for this competition, she was sure she had done her best in Birmingham.

Unfortunately, it was not good enough and Michelle placed fourth. Lu Chen was the gold medalist, while Surya Bonaly placed second, and Nicole Bobek took third.

Michelle was disappointed, but a few days later she figured out why she didn't place higher. It seemed that many of the judges thought she still skated like a child. She had to work harder at becoming more artistic on the ice, and she and Frank decided to change her little girl image. Even though Michelle was only 14, she needed to look older. Michelle always wore a pony tail, which made her look younger. Frank was convinced that she would improve her scores if she wore makeup and styled her hair differently. "I guess I've never seen an Olympic or world champion look like a little girl," she told one reporter. "Oksana Baiul, even though she was 15, looked glamorous."

Michelle's parents were not pleased about the makeover plan, however. "I'll be 15 and just like any other 15-year-old, I want to dress and look differently than I did when I was, say, 13," Michelle said to a reporter. "That's why I'm going for a little more sophisticated look—on and off the ice." Finally, Danny and Estella agreed that it might help her scores if she played up the artistic, rather than the athletic, aspect of figure skating.

In the meantime, Michelle toured with Brian Boitano, who gave her advice and coached her in their spare time. In between appearances, Michelle returned to Lake Arrowhead, where she and Karen stayed with their mother. Ron, meanwhile, was away at college. Danny had taken early retirement from the telephone company, but he still spent a lot of time at the Golden Pheasant in Torrance.

As Michelle worked on altering her image, her growing body was also changing. As she got taller and gained weight, there was concern that her skating would also be affected and that the changes would interfere with how she moved on the ice. Michelle knew better, however. As she started to prepare for the 1996 Nationals, she worked with Frank and her choreographer, Lori Nichol, to put together all of the pieces of her performance. Preparations took a while, but finally Frank had an idea that really worked. Michelle debuted her new image at the Skate America competition in October 1995, a few months before the 1996 Worlds.

She skated to the music of *Salome,* an opera written by German composer Richard Strauss. Strauss had adapted his work from the biblical story in which the character Salome performs the dance of seven veils. To fit the part, Michelle styled her hair in a chignon—a twist on the back of her head near her neck. She wore plenty of makeup and bright red lipstick. This was certainly a different Michelle than most people expected, and she felt her new image was perfect for the 1996 Nationals in San Jose, Texas.

Michelle spun and swirled into the competition with a triple-lutz double-toe loop combination. As Salome, her moves flowed perfectly with Strauss's music, and the judges were impressed. They gave her all first-place scores. Smiling and crying at the same time, Michelle accepted her gold medal. She had achieved her first Nationals win, and she didn't feel like a kid anymore.

Still, knowing that the World Championships would be difficult, Michelle could not really relax. She would be skating against the

defending champion Lu Chen of China. One of the favorites at the Worlds that year in Edmonton, Canada, Michelle did well on her short program, getting the best scores from the judges. She knew, however, that she would not win the competition based only on that program. In the end, the long program would be the deciding factor.

Scheduled to skate last, Michelle waited through Lu Chen's long program, during which the young Chinese skater performed six perfect triple jumps. When Michelle and Frank heard the thundering applause as Lu Chen finished her program, they knew that she had done very well. They also knew what that meant for

A significant part of Michelle's preparation for the 1996 Nationals involved the element of dance in her routines. Here she works with a professional choreographer to perfect her style and movements.

Elegance and grace are hallmarks of Michelle's performances. She excels in both the short programs and free skating, as she shows here during a qualifying round for the Nationals.

Michelle: she would have to skate a near perfect program to win the gold.

Michelle went for it. Again, she performed as Salome, gliding effortlessly across the ice. She knew that every move needed to be right if she was to have a chance at taking home the gold. At the last minute, Michelle added an inspired seventh triple jump—at a spot in her program where she had only planned to do a double. In the end, it may have been that move that made the difference. By the time her program was finished, Michelle was crying. She knew she had excelled.

"The crowd was great," she told a reporter. "[E]veryone was on their feet and the emotions took over and I knew I did it." In the end, the judges gave her two 6.0s and seven 5.9s. Michelle cried again when she saw her scores. She was the new world figure skating champion. At last, she was in the same class as Brian Boitano and her other heroes. For the third time that day, tears overwhelmed Michelle as she stood on the podium and accepted her gold medal.

Scarcely able to believe it, Michelle kept telling herself over and over that she was the world champion. In one year, Michelle had become the best female figure skater in the world.

7

SILVER MEDALIST
WITH A HEART OF GOLD

Fame has its ups and downs—just like Michelle's life. Elated with her championship win in 1996, she spent the next 11 months winning numerous competitions around the world. At times, however, the excitement of being a champion skater was overwhelming. Reporters begged her for interviews, and she was sought after for television talk shows. Everyone was convinced that Michelle would be the next Olympic gold medalist.

Michelle's whole life had changed in the last few years. Her parents moved into a house at Lake Arrowhead, and Ron and Karen were away at college. Suddenly her best friend, Karen, was far away in Boston. Also, a good friend and supporter of Michelle's, Harris Collins, died that year. Michelle felt very alone with all the changes in her life.

Still, she started the 1997 skating season by winning two more gold medals—one at a competition called the Ultimate Four and one at the Skate America Tournament—and *Skating* magazine had twice named her Skater of the Year. Michelle's usual gusto for skating was gone, however.

At the top of her sport and with an often hectic schedule, Michelle still has time to take part in other ventures. In conjunction with Walt Disney Television Network, Michelle is part of an Internet promotion to involve fans in selecting songs for upcoming Disney specials in which Michelle will participate.

When she was on the ice, she did not feel as excited as she once had, and her feelings affected her performances during the 1997 U.S. Championships and World Championships.

At the U.S. competition in Nashville, Tennessee, Michelle did fine in her short program, but thousands of television viewers watched her fall three times during her long program. By the time she finished, she was thoroughly embarrassed by her performance. For the first time in nearly a year, Michelle had not won a competition. Although she took home the silver medal, Tara Lipinski, who was only 14 years old, captured the gold.

Despite her loss, Michelle still qualified for the world competition in Switzerland. Reporters were writing that she and Tara would be in a duel for the gold medal, and Michelle knew she needed to work especially hard.

As the Worlds got underway, Michelle missed a jump in her short program. Although she continued skating, she began to cry, worried that she would again fail to win the gold medal. When she finished her short program, she was ranked fourth.

During the next few days, before she performed her long program, former Olympic skater Scott Hamilton announced that he had cancer. At the same time, Carlo Fassi, another coach who Michelle knew, unexpectedly died while in Switzerland. For Michelle, these sudden tragedies made a skating competition seem far less important by comparison. She realized that fourth place was not so bad and that things could be much worse.

With a renewed spirit, Michelle sailed across the ice for her long program without any mistakes, winning the long competition.

Her leg in a cast from a stress fracture, Michel smiles when international champion Micha Chack autographs the cast. Michelle's early 1997 season saw som poor performances, including several falls, but she recovered her confidence and renew her dedication to winni Olympic gold.

However, her short program scores had hurt her overall standing. She graciously accepted the silver medal and watched Tara collect the gold.

Michelle had learned a valuable life's lesson, telling a reporter for *Sports Illustrated*:

> I'm glad last year [1997] happened. . . .
> I didn't appreciate what I'd already done.
> I didn't enjoy it. I was so worried about
> winning. . . . I kept asking myself, "Why am
> I here if I don't love it?" . . . It's supposed to
> be fun, and I thought I'd die if I didn't win.

It may not have been a fortunate year for skating, but Michelle had grown as a person.

She was now a mature skater and a stronger young women.

Nearly a year later when Michelle glided onto the ice in Philadelphia for the 1998 National Championships, she again showed the world that skating was meant to be fun. She had bounced from a low point in her life back to the top. That meant, however, that the pressure was on going into the 1998 Olympics in Nagano.

When the soft lyrical music of "Lyra Angelica" signaled Michelle's performance, a hushed silence filled the Olympic arena as the crowd watched Michelle perform. All seven of her triple jumps were clean and solid. She skated with style, grace, and most of all, joy. At the end, the audience burst into wild applause and threw bouquets of flowers onto the ice.

Michelle felt she did well on her long program, but she was unsure if she had been good enough to win the gold. When her free skate ended, she burst into tears—tears of joy and relief—and rushed to where her mother waited to see her final scores. The judges gave her presentation all 5.9s, but her technical merit scores were not as high: five were 5.7s and four were 5.8s. Even though Michelle knew the audience supported her, she felt it might be almost impossible to surpass the high standards she had set at the Nationals in Philadelphia.

One by one, Michelle watched each of the other skaters take their turns, including Tara Lipinski, who skated next to last. Tara's moves were exceptional, and in the end, Michelle fell just short of grasping the gold medal by what seemed to be just one jump. The difference between her performance and Tara's was a triple—triple combination, which requires a skater to repeat two triple jumps in succession.

Michelle did not perform any triple—triples. Three of the Olympic judges thought she was the best skater, but six of them favored Tara.

At the awards ceremony, Michelle hugged and kissed her medal-winning teammate. Together, they were the first pair of U.S. skaters to take first and second place in the singles division since 1956. Smiling graciously, Michelle stood on the second-place platform. She had come for the gold, but a second-place finish was nearly as good. Proudly she wore her silver medal and smiled through her tears while the "Star Spangled Banner" was played. "I can walk away really happy," Michelle told reporters at a press conference after the event. "Because it's *c'est la vie*, right? [*C'est la vie* means "that's life" in French.] Even though you work really hard it doesn't mean you'll get the gold."

Michelle's fans admired her gracious behavior toward her teammate Tara, and many still tell her they're disappointed that she missed the gold medal. Some of them even burst into tears. "It was the hardest moment of my life," Michelle told a reporter from *Newsweek* a year later. "I was so close to what I'd always dreamed of that I could taste it. Afterwards, I just tried to hold it together. But when I saw my dad and mom, I lost it. They wanted it for me more than even I did."

Frank worried that everyone who consoled Michelle would make her think that she really had deserved the gold medal. He knew she could skate better than she did at the Olympics, and he decided to try and spur her on to want the gold even more. He challenged the dispirited young skater. "I knew it might even jeopardize our future together," he told a *Newsweek* reporter. "But if she listened to others, she might feel she got screwed out of the gold and have been bitter for the rest of her life. So I took her aside and said, `You were too slow and too tentative—you didn't let go.' She knew it."

Michelle too commented when asked about losing the Olympic gold. "A couple hours of your life is not everything," she told a *People* magazine reporter. "You shouldn't let it determine whether you'll have success and happiness."

After Nagano, Michelle returned to the United States and won her next 11 competitions, including the 1998 Worlds. Frequently, she received perfect scores. In 1999, however, at the Worlds in Helsinki, Finland, Michelle placed second to Maria Butyrskaya of Russia, who took the gold. Again, Michelle accepted her silver medal with grace and dignity.

Michelle's coach said she was recuperating from a cold and that may have affected her practices prior to the competition. "The cold probably hit harder mentally, than physically," Michelle herself told a reporter from the *Chicago Tribune* after the competition. "At the beginning of the week I was pretty confident, but I was fighting with the cold and my confidence level went down."

It takes a lot to get Michelle down. She has won more awards in the last decade than any other figure skater in the world, grasping the gold at 26 events, including two world and three U.S. championships. Much of her skating is nearly perfect as well. To date she has received 39 perfect 6.0 marks from skating judges.

In 1998 Michelle concluded a deal with the Walt Disney Network to skate in various television specials. Her first performance was in an ice spectacular to celebrate Disney's animated feature film *Mulan*. Called *Reflections on Ice:*

As part of her contract with Disney, Michelle skated the role of Mulan in the television special Reflections on Ice. *She was joined by an impressive cast that included championship skaters and a huge cast of ice acrobats.*

Michelle appears with Michael Eisner (right), chairman of the Walt Disney Company, and publisher Steve Murphy (left). Her contract with Disney includes television skating specials, and with Murphy, she is authoring children's books.

Michelle Kwan Skates to the Music of Disney's Mulan—Michelle played the lead role of the young and courageous Chinese princess Mulan, who becomes a warrior and fights to protect her family's honor. Delighted to take part, Michelle was drawn to the film's song "Reflection." "I was particularly touched by the song 'Reflection,'" she said, "and the minute I heard it I knew that I wanted to skate to it."

Yet, the Olympic silver medalist with the heart of gold has managed to squeeze much more than just skating into her busy life. She has hosted prime-time TV skating specials, written her autobiography, and even stars in her own interactive video game called Michelle Kwan Figure Skating. In addition, she is the national spokesperson for the Children's Miracle Network Champions Across America program and was the 1999 national chairperson for Teen Read Week. She was so busy that she even had to turn down an offer to visit President Bill Clinton at the White House.

Although "work hard, be yourself, and have fun" is still Michelle's skating philosophy, it appears it has also become her motto for life. In 1998 she received her high school diploma with a grade-point average of 3.61. In 1999 she received the Dial Award given to the top graduating athlete in the country.

She took time off in the winter of 1999 to visit Hawaii and spend time with her family. While she was there she enjoyed parasailing, tennis, and scuba diving and thought hard about her plans for the future. "I want to go to college," she told a reporter from the *Chicago Tribune.* "I hear from my sister how wonderful it is, how it is a new life, a different sort of life than skating, skating, skating."

Eventually, Michelle chose the University of California at Los Angeles (UCLA), and because she wanted to get to know lots of different people, she decided to live in a dorm. "I don't even know anyone who isn't a skater," she told a *Newsweek* reporter. "I want to get to know people my age who have other goals."

As she explained to another reporter:

> Ever since seventh or eighth grade, I've had private tutors and never really had the chance to meet other students. I decided to go all out with college, stay in the dorms, meet other people. I just want to be a normal student. . . . I want the whole experience I missed out on in high school.

Nineteen-year-old Michelle also has her own home in Lake Arrowhead, right next door to her parent's house.

Attending college while continuing to skate is yet another challenge in her young life. Even though Michelle is looking ahead to her future, she still works hard at her skating. She tries to practice every morning before classes as well as on weekends back at Lake Arrowhead. Several weekends after school started, she traveled to ice skating competitions around the country. At the Keri Lotion Figure Skating Classic in Orlando, Florida, she took home a gold medal, defeating world champion Maria Butyrskaya.

"At times I think, 'Why should I push myself all those long hours in the rink?'" she commented to a *Newsweek* reporter. "But then I think, 'How will I ever know how good I could have been?' I want to be the Michael Jordan of my sport."

Michelle is still a favorite for the Salt Lake City Olympics in 2002. Even while attending college, she talks about practicing hard and designing more difficult programs. She plans to go for the Olympic gold again, and it seems as though she may not give up until she has it.

CHRONOLOGY

1980   Born July 7 to Estella and Danny Kwan in Torrance, California

1986   Begins skating

1987   Enters her first figure skating competition

1988   Watches Brian Boitano win an Olympic gold medal on TV

1990   Begins training with her sister, Karen, at Ice Castle in Lake Arrowhead, California, under the direction of Coach Frank Carroll

1992   Ranks ninth at Junior National competition; passes the test to qualify for senior competitions

1993   Finishes sixth at the U.S. National Championships; wins the gold medal at the World Junior Championships

1994   Wins the silver medal at the U.S. National Championships; places eighth at the World Championships; ranks second at both the Pro-Am Games and the Goodwill Games; goes to the Olympics in Lillehammer, Norway, as an alternate but does not compete

1995   Wins the silver medal at the U.S. National Championships; places forth in the World Championships

1996   Wins the gold medal at the U.S. National Championships and the World Championships

1997   Beaten by Tara Lipinski in both the U.S. National Championships and the World Championships

1998   Wins the silver medal at the Olympics in Nagano, Japan; places first in World competition a few weeks later and wins 10 straight competitions; graduates from high school; signs with Walt Disney for TV specials

1999   Wins the U.S. National Championships; places second at Worlds to Russian skater Maria Butyrskaya; begins attending college at UCLA

2000   Signs $1 million endorsement deal with Chevrolet; wins the U.S. National Championships and the World Championships

ACCOMPLISHMENTS

Championship Wins

1993 Southwest Pacific Senior
      Competition
      Pacific Coast Senior Competition
      U.S. Olympic Festival

1994 World Junior Championships
      U.S. Outdoor Challenge

1995 International Challenge
      Skate America
      Skate Canada
      Nations Cup

1996 U.S. National Championships
      (Senior)
      Champion Series Final
      World Championships
      Continents Cup
      Skate America
      Trophee Lalique
      Ultimate Four

1997 Japan Open
      Skate America
      Skate Canada

1998 U.S. National Championships
      World Championships
      Ultimate Four
      Goodwill Games
      Figure Skating Classic
      Grand Slam of Skating
      U.S. Pro Classic
      Masters of Skating
      World Pro

1999 Japan Open
      U.S. National Championships
      Keri Lotion Figure Skating
      Classic

2000 U.S. National Championships
      World Championships

FURTHER READING

Epstein, Edward Z. *Born to Skate: The Michelle Kwan Story.* New York: Ballantine Books, 1997.

Gatto, Kimberly. *Michelle Kwan: Champion on Ice.* Minneapolis: Lerner Publications, 1998.

Kwan, Michelle, as told to Linda James. *Heart of a Champion.* New York: Scholastic, 1997.

Kwan, Michelle. *My Book of Memories.* New York: Scholastic, 1998.

Kwan, Michelle, as told to Linda James. *The Winning Attitude.* New York: Hyperion, 1999.

Lovitt, Chip. *Skating for the Gold: Tara Lipinski and Michelle Kwan.* New York: Pocket Books, 1997.

Shaughnessy, Linda. *Michelle Kwan: Skating Like the Wind.* Parsippany, NJ: Silver Burdett Press, 1997.

Torres, John Albert. *Michelle Kwan.* Elkton, MD: Mitchell Lane Publishers, 1999.

Wellman, Sam. *Michelle Kwan.* Philadelphia: Chelsea House Publishers, 1998.

ABOUT THE AUTHOR

SHERRY BECK PAPROCKI is a freelance journalist who has written for the *Chicago Tribune*, the *Los Angeles Times Syndicate*, the *Cleveland Plain Dealer*, and many more publications. She has written one other book for children, *Easy Microwave Cooking for Kids*, and has contributed to several others. She resides near Columbus, Ohio, with her husband and their two children.

HANNAH STORM, NBC Sports play-by-play announcer, reporter, and studio host, made her debut in 1992 at Wimbledon during the All England Tennis Championships. Shortly thereafter, she was paired with Jim Lampley to cohost the *Olympic Show* for the 1992 Olympic Games in Barcelona. Later that year, Storm was named cohost of *Notre Dame Saturday*, NBC's college football pregame show. Adding to her repertoire, Storm became a reporter for the 1994 Major League All-Star Game and the pregame host for the 1995, 1997, and 1999 World Series. Storm's success as host of *NBA Showtime* during the 1997-98 season won her the role as studio host for the inaugural season of the Women's National Basketball Association in 1998.

In 1996, Storm was selected as NBC's host for the Summer Olympics in Atlanta, and she has been named as host for both the 2000 Summer Olympics in Sydney and the 2002 Winter Olympics in Salt Lake City. Storm received a Gracie Allen Award for Outstanding Personal Achievement, which was presented by the American Women in Radio and Television Foundation (AWRTF), for her coverage of the 1999 NBA Finals and 1999 World Series. She has been married to NBC Sports broadcaster Dan Hicks since 1994. They have two daughters.

INDEX